STALLION EDITIONS

THE 8 RULES OF
THE GRAND GAME OF LIFE

STALLION EDITIONS

Copyright © 2024 Matt Dispa
All rights reserved.

Published by Stallion Editions

ISBN 978-87-85259-00-4

sites.google.com/view/stallion-editions

Printed in Denmark

MATT DISPA

The 8 Rules
of the Grand Game of Life

A Beginner's Guide to a Life of Abundance

At the beginning, it is just an idea.

It is only in your MIND.

Then it appears on the paper.

Finally, it becomes a reality.

INTRODUCTION

This short book will teach you how to get the body you want.
The money you want.
The car you want.
The house you want.

If you get all this, I bet you won't be fully satisfied if you don't get the relationships that you want. Healthy and beautiful relationships to your loved ones, your spouse, your parents and your children, are one of the most important things in life. That's why this book will also teach you to get the relationships you dream of, with the partner your dream of and the family you dream of.

Imagine that, once again, you get all of that.
There is still a chance that some of you won't feel truly happy and blessed. Most of us often climb all the way to the top and seem to have it all, but within us, something might still be missing. Most of us spend years building but we let everything collapse when the vicissitudes of life strike us.
That's why this book will also teach you to be grateful and loving no matter your circumstances. To be balanced and grounded even if you're standing on shaky ground.

Yes, you can have it all.
Be happy, healthy, wealthy.
Successful in all areas of life.
You can be a winner in the Grand Game of Life.
But how? you might ask.

It's quite simple.
First, by becoming aware of the rules which govern your existence and the world you live in.
There are 8 of them.
Secondly, by understanding these 8 rules and using them to your advantage to create a life of abundance.
Finally, by creating your own rules and designing the life you've always dreamed to live.

In the Grand Game of Life, we are all players with the power to shape our destiny. The 8 rules are our guideposts, illuminating the path to a deeper understanding of the world and of ourselves.
They are the keys to unlock the fullness of our potential and achieve true success.

As you navigate the Game of Life, remember these rules, and let them guide you towards a life of endless possibilities.

Welcome to the Grand Game of Life.
Let's start playing.

RULE 1

"Life is a Game we are all playing."

The first rule is that Life itself is a game, and we are its players. I'm not trying to prove to you here that life is some sort of VR, video game or Matrix you are *really* plugged into.

That would be irrelevant.

My point is that I want you to consider the Grand Game of Life as a possibility. I want you to play with that powerful idea, to explore it, to experiment with it and eventually to see for yourself if that idea has the power to change your life for the better.

When discovering a new idea, most people keep asking themselves : "Is it true? Is it true? Is it true?" And they start an investigation to figure out if their hypothesis will turn true or false. Even though I agree that the quest for Truth is one of the most meaningful thing one can pursue in life, I often replace the question "Is it true?" by another one :

"Is it going to benefit me?"
Is believing in this new idea going to improve my life?
Is it going to make me a better person? Is it going to make me a happier, more fulfilled or more balanced person?

Is believing in this new theory going to help me achieve my goals and live a better, healthier, richer life?
Is it going to benefit the people I care about?

You bet, if I discover a new idea that will help me on my journey to an abundant life, I will get emotionally involved with it. And I adopt it.

On the contrary, if that new idea is going to make me scared, angry, distrustful or unhappy, I will simply leave it behind.

Moreover, if an idea is destructive or harmful to me or my loved ones, I will without hesitation make the choice to not get emotionally involved with it, to not give it any attention, or even to protect myself from it, and basically forget about it.

Like an architect choosing the best material to build an edifice and discarding low quality material that could compromise its strength and beauty.

Let's have a quick overview of the idea of Life as a game.
Take a moment to picture Life as an elaborate game, brimming with levels, challenges, upgrades and rewards, and endless opportunities for growth.
Think of Life as an immense cosmic game all beings are playing. Each decision, each action, is a move of the game.
Our real-life choices shape our journey.
And define our destiny.

Imagine for a second that since the day you were born,
you've been a part of that game, but without being aware of it.
You were given a hand of cards.
Everyone expected you to make the best of it.
But no one told you the rules of the game.
No one told you how to play these cards.
In other words, no one taught you neither about the existence of the game nor how to play it.

Can you imagine a Monopoly game in which you were involved since your youngest age, investing real time, energy and money, and the consequences of that game would determine all the parameters of your life?
But... you were not aware of it.

Even worse, you were ignorant of its most basic rules.

Do you think you would stand a chance against other players if they had fully understood the game and its most intricate functions? Or, without even comparing yourself to others, do you think you would be in a position to make the most of it?

Absolutely not.

Let me guess.
Ever since your birth, you have probably been navigating your life by trial and error, sometimes with success and sometimes with failure, maybe blessed by happiness at times or doomed by despair at others, but without fully understanding what that immensely complex experience we call Life was all about.
This is about to change.

Today, the Game has started.
Let's give it our best shot.
Let's play to win, grow and thrive.

Life, in its essence, is a complex and dynamic interplay of actions, reactions and consequences.
Life is a Game we are all playing.
Not only Life is a Game, it is the Ultimate Game.

A game that can end at any moment, which makes every second precious. An unpredictable game, with rules that can change without warning.

It doesn't take place on a board or a screen.

It is happening on the entire planet.

In other words, the Universe is our playground.

And the main character is YOU.

From the space stations in orbit around the Earth to the indigenous tribes of remote lands, from the busyness of great cities to the calm of the deepest forests, there is an infinity of players just like you, every single one of them being unique and influencing all the others, directly or undirectly, every choice they make, every action they take, having a ripple effect through space and time. And the parameters of the Game, as well as the possibilities offered to its players, are endless.

Every decision we make, every challenge we face, and every opportunity we seize are moves on the chess game that will have consequences, good or bad, and that will create an infinity of other choices and opportunities.

Each second of each day, we navigate through a series of actions, may they be big or small, seeming insignificant or of extreme importance, all of which shape our journey and define our experience of life.

In your life, external factors may influence your journey, but it is your determination, hard work and perseverance that will be the true drivers of success. With the right mindset and effort, you can turn your visions and dreams into reality.

Therefore, how well we play the Game will decide of the Life we will live. Happy or unhappy, healthy or sick, rich or poor.

Only a few know of its existence and are familiar with its rules. Most people are totally unaware of it.

Those who ignore the rules of the Game, or worse, who are unaware of their own participation, reduce dramatically their chances of success.

The ones who realize the existence of the Game, and who uncover the secrets of its rules, will have an unfair advantage. Because in the Grand Game of Life, knowledge is power.

By now being aware of the Game of Life, and by learning its rules, you can transform your approach to your own journey, overcome obstacles, and create a life that is purposeful, rich and immensely rewarding.

The better you understand the existing rules, the better equipped you are to navigate the complexities of your own existence and design the life that you've always wanted, the life which aligns with your values and dreams.

You will soon discover that your own potential is not limited but infinite, because the possibilities within the Grand Game of Life are limitless.

Therefore, dream big, take risks, and pursue your passions with confidence and determination.

If you simply push beyond your self-imposed limits, you will achieve extraordinary things.

Who knows what you're capable of?

Anything and everything.

RULE 2

"The Game can end anytime."

The impermanence of life
is a stark reminder of its preciousness.

You didn't expect that, did you?
Starting with the end of the Game.
Beginning with Death to talk about Life.

Well, that's probably because Life and Death are so intricately connected. They are necessary opposites.
You can't have one without the other.

There is not light without darkness. No yin without yang.
No positive without negative.

And you won't be able to play any game well, if you're not aware of its end.

Life, that exquisite and perplexing game, holds within it an ultimate and undeniable truth: the Game can end anytime. Without notice, without warning, the curtain can fall, leaving behind only echoes of our existence.

No one knows the day or the hour, but there is an end to the Game for every single one of us. This amazing game called Life can finish anytime. So enjoy it to the fullest with every cell of your body for every second that it lasts.

This rule, often shrouded in the shadows of our everyday awareness, urges us to embrace life with a profound sense of presence and joy, to savor every moment as a precious gift. For in recognizing the impermanence of our being, we unlock the true essence of living.

From the moment we draw our first breath, we are set on a path that will eventually lead to our last. We didn't chose to enter the Game the day we were born, and we won't chose to exit it the day we die. This journey, unpredictable and often beyond our control, is marked by a series of beginnings and endings. Every experience, every relationship, and every achievement is transient, existing within the bounds of time. Yet we often live as if we were eternal. As if there was always a tomorrow to fulfill our dreams, mend our mistakes or express our love.

In Life, this illusion of permanence can be both a comfort and a trap. It lulls us into complacency, making us forget the fleeting nature of our existence. But by embracing the truth that the Game can end at any moment, we transcend this illusion and live with a heightened awareness and appreciation for the present.

To fully engage in the Grand Game of Life, we must learn to be present. This means immersing ourselves in the HERE and NOW, experiencing each moment with full awareness and attention. It is in the present that Life truly unfolds, where we find the richness of our existence and the beauty of our experiences.

Take a deep breath, relax.
And then fully focus on the next following lines.

HERE is the only place you'll ever be.
There is no THERE.
NOW is the only time that ever was and ever will be.
There is no past, and no future.
NOW is everything there is, everything that ever was,
and everything that ever will be.
Everything is HERE and NOW.
Anything else is an illusion.

This practice of presence is not about denying the past or ignoring the future. It is about recognizing that the past is a memory, the future a projection, and that our true reality lies in the present moment.

By living in the NOW, we honor the transient nature of Life and make the most of the time we are granted.

Imagine savoring a meal, not merely for its nourishment but for the symphony of flavors, the texture, the aroma. Consider a conversation with a loved one, not as a routine exchange of words but as a profound connection, a sharing of souls. By anchoring ourselves in the present, we transform the mundane into the magical, the ordinary into the extraordinary.

The uncertainty of when the Game will end is, paradoxically, one of Life's greatest gifts. It is this uncertainty that imbues our experiences with urgency and significance. If we knew exactly when our time would come, we might be tempted to postpone our dreams, delay our actions or take our relationships for granted.

But the very uncertainty of Life's duration compels us to live fully and authentically. This gift of uncertainty encourages us to pursue our passions, take risks, and embrace opportunities. It reminds us that Life is too short for regrets, that we should strive to create memories and leave a legacy that reflects our true selves. It prompts us to love, to forgive, to seek adventure and to cherish the people and moments that matter most.

Often, the easiest way to focus on what is the most important, is to let go of everything else.

Clinging to the past, harboring grudges or fixating on future anxieties only distracts us from our ability to live fully in the present. Letting go does not mean forgetting or dismissing our experiences, but rather acknowledging them, learning from them, and then moving forward with grace and acceptance.

This practice of letting go is essential for our emotional and mental well-being. It frees us from the chains of regret and fear, allowing us to navigate Life with a lighter heart and an open mind. It enables us to appreciate the beauty of the present without being weighed down by the burdens of the past or the uncertainties of the future.

Moreover, when we embrace the notion that Life can end at any moment, we cultivate a profound sense of gratitude. Each day, each breath, becomes a precious gift, an opportunity to experience the wonders of existence. Gratitude shifts our focus from what we lack to what we have, from our struggles to our blessings.

Living with gratitude means acknowledging the abundance in our lives, no matter how small or insignificant it may seem.

It means appreciating the simple pleasures—a sunrise, a smile, a moment of silence, the wind caressing your face. It means recognizing the people who enrich our lives and the experiences that shape our journey.

Gratitude also fosters resilience, helping us to navigate Life's challenges with a positive outlook. It reminds us that even in the face of adversity, there is always something to be thankful for. By cultivating gratitude, we enhance our capacity for joy and contentment, making the most of the time given to us.

Let's do something together.
Let's play.

Take a deep breath.
Be aware of the air entering your lungs.

Now imagine that this Life of yours, however great or small, happy or unhappy, filled with all the people you know, the experiences you've done and the memories you've made, that Life will end in a month from now.

Think about it.

Be aware of how it would feel if you knew that in a month's time, everything will be over.

Embody and embrace what it would feel like.

What would you do?
What would you plan for your last month on Earth?

What would you prioritize to make the most of it?
Take the time to reflect upon that idea.

Now, let's move on.
Let's think about how it would feel if you had, not one month, but one day left. How would that be?

How would you spend your last day?

Out of a place of peace and gratitude, focus on what would be the most important to you on that last day.
Take the time to let all your emotions sink in.

Once again, let's move on.
You don't have a day left. You have one minute left.
Only a minute. Such a brief time.

What would then be the most important to you during that one last minute?
What would you focus on? How would you feel?
Take the time to truly be aware of how you would appreciate and enjoy these last precious seconds of life.

Finally, I want you to stay focused on that last feeling, "the *Last Minute* feeling", and I'm going to ask something of you. Something very important.

I want you to try to live the rest of your life, this unknown number of extremely precious seconds, with the same feeling than if you were living the very last ones of them.

I want you to live every minute like if it was your last.

For a lot of people who go through this exercise, this mental yoga, knowing that the game can end anytime reminds them to cherish the HERE and NOW, everything they see, hear, smell, taste and touch.

But very often, it also makes them cherish the people in their lives, nurture their connections, and express their love and appreciation. The transient nature of Life underscores the importance of our relationships. Because relationships are the threads that weave the fabric of our existence, providing support, joy and meaning.

Being fully present in our interactions with others deepens our connections and enriches our relationships. It sometimes means listening with empathy, speaking with honesty, and acting with kindness. It means valuing the time we spend with loved ones, creating memories that will endure forever.

Because ultimately, the awareness that the game can end anytime inspires us to consider the legacy we leave behind. Our actions and choices will keep shaping the world long after we are gone. The impact we have on others, the contributions we make and the memories we create, form our enduring legacy.

Living with this awareness encourages us to act with integrity, to be mindful of our influence, and to strive for a positive and lasting impact. It prompts us to share our wisdom, to mentor and support others, and to contribute to the betterment of our communities and the world at large.

Our legacy is not just about grand achievements or monumental accomplishments. It is also about the small, everyday acts of kindness, the love we share, and the joy we bring to others. It is about living a life that is true to our values, reflects our deepest aspirations, and leaves the world a better place.

Therefore the awareness that the Game of Life will end is not a cause for fear or despair but an invitation to live fully and authentically. It urges us to embrace the present, to cultivate gratitude and joy, to nurture our relationships, and to seek meaning and purpose.

By recognizing the impermanence of existence, we unlock the true essence of living. We learn to savor each moment, to let go of what no longer serves us and to create a life that is rich, fulfilling, and deeply meaningful.

Let's play the Grand Game of Life with presence and passion, and with the understanding that every second is a precious gift we should constantly cherish.

RULE 3

"The rules of the Game can change anytime."

Can you imagine a game that would have not only an infinite set of rules, but that these very rules would be changing as the game goes? What a wild game that would be!
That is nonetheless the game you play everyday of your life.

Let me take an example.
Let's pretend you are a professional athlete.
Your physical abilities are extraordinary, and they allow you to live in luxury and happiness.
One day though, you have a car accident and lose the use of your legs. Within seconds, the rules of your life have changed radically and forever.
It is the same when you lose someone.
It is the same if an earthquake hits the area you live in.
Suddenly, without warning, without notice, you can't play by the same rules. You can't play the same game.
That is why, no matter your situation and circumstances, you should always be adaptable.

Life, in its boundless complexity and inherent unpredictability, is a dance of ever-shifting rules. We are on this journey with a set of beliefs, expectations and habits, only to find that the Game can change anytime.
Without warning, without notice, our circumstances can drastically alter, compelling us to adapt constantly, grow, and transcend our previous understanding.

This realization invites us to embrace the fluidity of existence, to navigate the waves of change with grace, and to find harmony in the midst of chaos.

Change is the very essence of Life. From the moment we are born to the instant we take our last breath, we are in a constant state of flux. Our body adapts, our mind expands, our environment transforms.

Yet, despite this inherent dynamism, we often cling to the illusion of stability and permanence. Our brain builds routines, establishes norms and constructs narratives that offer a semblance of control and predictability.

However, Life, in its infinite wisdom, continuously reminds us of its impermanent nature. The unforeseen opportunity, the unexpected job loss, the sudden illness—each event disrupts our carefully crafted plans and forces us to confront the reality that the rules of the Game can change at any moment.

Embracing this truth is both a challenge and a liberation, as it compels us to let go of our rigid expectations and cultivate a mindset of openness and resilience.

Consider the weather—a metaphor for Life's unpredictability. We can forecast, predict and plan, but we cannot control the storms or the sunshine.

Similarly, we can set goals, make decisions and take action, but we must also be prepared to adapt to unforeseen changes. Recognizing the illusion of absolute control liberates us from the burden of perfectionism and the fear of failure, allowing us to engage with Life more authentically and spontaneously.

To navigate the ever-changing rules of the Game, we must learn to embrace uncertainty. This means cultivating a mindset that is comfortable with the unknown, that sees change not as a threat but as an opportunity for growth and discovery.

Embracing uncertainty involves letting go of our need for security, and instead, developing trust in the process of Life.

Trusting the process means having faith in our ability to adapt and respond to whatever comes our way. It means recognizing that every challenge carries within it the seeds of growth and transformation.

When we embrace uncertainty, we open ourselves to new possibilities and experiences, allowing Life to unfold in ways that we could never have imagined.

In the face of changing rules, our greatest ally is our capacity for adaptation. Adaptation is the ability to adjust our thoughts, behaviors, and strategies in response to new circumstances. It is a dynamic process that requires flexibility, creativity and resilience.

Adaptation begins with awareness—recognizing that change is occurring and understanding its implications. This awareness allows us to respond proactively rather than reactively. It involves assessing the new situation, identifying potential challenges and opportunities, and adjusting our approach accordingly.

Flexibility is the cornerstone of adaptation.

It means being willing to let go of old habits, beliefs and strategies that no longer serve us. It means being open to new perspectives, learning new skills and exploring new paths. Flexibility allows us to flow with the changing currents of Life rather than resisting them.

Creativity is another vital component of adaptation. When the rules of the Game change, we are often called upon to find innovative solutions and think outside the box. Creativity enables us to see possibilities where others see obstacles, to turn challenges into opportunities and to forge new paths when the old ones are no longer viable.

Attachment to the familiar, to our expectations and to our desires is often the source of our suffering in the face of change. When the rules of the Game shift, our attachment to the old rules can create resistance and distress.

Letting go of attachment is not about abandoning our goals or desires but about releasing our rigid expectations, embracing the fluid nature of Life and finding alternative ways to reach our goals. Letting go involves accepting that change, just like birth and death, is a natural and inevitable part of existence. It means acknowledging that our current circumstances, no matter how comfortable or secure, are temporary.
By letting go of attachment, we free ourselves from the constraints of the past and open ourselves to the possibilities of the present and the future.

But keep in mind the previous rule.

In a world where the rules can change at any moment, presence in the HERE and NOW is our anchor. Presence is the necessary condition to be fully engaged and experience life as it unfolds. It is about immersing ourselves in the present moment, without being distracted by the past or anxious about the future.

Presence allows us to respond to change with clarity and equanimity. When we are present, we are more attuned to the nuances of our environment, more aware of the subtle shifts and signals that indicate change. This heightened awareness enables us to adapt more effectively and to make decisions that are aligned with the current reality, no matter how quickly and brutally this reality has changed.

By practicing mindfulness, we develop a deeper awareness of our inner and outer worlds, enhancing our ability to navigate change with wisdom.
During or after traumatic experiences, we often feel ourselves drowning in a sense of chaos and uncertainty. In such times, finding balance is essential for our well-being and effectiveness.

Balance involves maintaining a sense of equilibrium amidst the fluctuations of Life, finding stability within ourselves even when our external circumstances are in flux.

Balance is also achieved through self-awareness and self-care. It means recognizing our physical, intellectual and spiritual needs and taking steps to meet them. It involves creating routines and practices that support our well-being, such as regular exercise, healthy eating and sufficient sleep.

Ultimately, the ever changing rules of the Game remind us of the wisdom of impermanence, the recognition that all things, both good and bad, are only temporary. This understanding can be a source of comfort and strength, as it teaches us that no situation is permanent, that change is a constant, and that we have the capacity to adapt and grow through it.

Impermanence encourages us to appreciate the present moment, to savor the beauty and joy of Life as it unfolds. It reminds us to cherish our relationships, to express our love and gratitude, and to find meaning in our daily experiences.

By embracing impermanence, we cultivate a deeper appreciation for the richness and diversity of Life.

Finally, the changing rules of the Game invite us to embrace the journey of Life in all its unpredictability and wonder.

Life is not a linear path but a dynamic and evolving adventure, full of twists and turns, discoveries and surprises.

By embracing the journey, we find joy and fulfillment in the process of living, rather than fixating on specific outcomes or destinations. As we navigate the ever-changing rules of the Game, we are reminded that Life is a dance, a fluid and dynamic interplay of forces and energies.

That is what makes it such a wonderful adventure.

Ask yourself, in full honesty :

"Would you really want to live a life that was a 100 % predictable? Would you like to live a life that was totally under your control?"

The truth is, even though there would be some fun in that to start with, a life that you would have entirely planned would quickly become boring, and eventually pointless.

Imagine for a second that you were a god in Heaven, blessed with omniscience and omnipotence for eternity, and that you could manifest absolutely anything with total control.

Sooner or later, you would be asking for a "surprise".

And what better surprise could you get than suddenly finding yourself living the life you are living today?

RULE 4

*"The rules of the Game are tools
not constraints."*

At the beginning, every one of us starts by learning the most basic rules of Life. Eating, walking, speaking, reading, writing. Later on, as we master the basics, the rules become more complex. Mathematics, literature, biology, chemistry, history, geography, finance, art, psychology, plus an infinity of others. A lot of people see this process of learning as a constraint or a burden.

In truth, they allow you to better understand the world you live in. And the deeper you understand the rules of the Game, the more able you will be one day at creating better ones.

Because the whole process of learning is not oppression, it is a liberation. You first have to identify the patterns that make our world what it is, then you learn to utilize them so finally, you can create your own patterns.

Take playing the piano, for example.
You don't start on day 1 by improvising a complex tune.
At the start, you begin by learning to identify the different notes. Then, you master simple tunes written by others. Over and over again. Ultimately, you'll be able to create you own, unique and beautiful masterpiece.

Learning is therefore a necessary condition to creation.

From our earliest moments, we begin to learn the rules that govern the Game. These foundational skills are the building blocks upon which we construct our understanding of the world. They are the tools that enable us to navigate our environment, communicate with others and express our thoughts and emotions.

Take the example of the act of walking. As infants, we observe those around us, tentatively taking our first steps, stumbling and falling, but gradually gaining confidence and proficiency. Quickly, walking becomes second nature, an automatic process that frees our minds to focus on more complex tasks. Similarly, speaking and language acquisition involve a process of imitation, experimentation and gradual mastery, allowing us to convey our ideas and connect with others. Reading and writing, once daunting challenges, become gateways to knowledge and imagination.

Through these skills, we access the collective wisdom of humanity, explore new worlds, and articulate our inner experiences. These foundational rules, though simple in their essence, are profound in their impact, shaping our cognitive and social development.

These rules, which at first seem fundamentally simple, gradually become more complex and nuanced as we grow. They guide our actions, shape our understanding and influence our interactions with the world. We delve into the realms of mathematics, literature, biology, chemistry, history, geography, finance, and so much more.

Each discipline offers a unique lens through which we can view and understand the world.

Mathematics teaches us the language of numbers and patterns, enabling us to solve problems and quantify our experiences. Literature invites us into the rich tapestry of human emotions and narratives, fostering empathy and creativity. Biology and chemistry reveal the intricate mechanisms of life, the interplay of molecules and organisms that sustain our existence. History and geography provide context, helping us to understand the forces that have shaped our world and our place within it. Finances and business introduce us to the principles of resource management, the dynamics of economies and the flow of money.

These disciplines, while seemingly disparate, are interconnected. They weave together a comprehensive understanding of the world, enabling us to see the bigger picture. By mastering these complex rules, we gain the ability to navigate Life with greater insight and intelligence.

We learn to recognize patterns, draw connections and make informed decisions.

It is easy to view the rules of Life as constraints, as burdens that limit our freedom and creativity.

Many of us don't even like the word "rule" anymore.

However, this perspective overlooks the true purpose of rules. Rules are not meant to confine us but to empower us. They provide structure and guidance, they are tools helping us to navigate the complexities of Life with clarity and purpose.

Imagine again a musician learning the scales and chords of their instrument. These basic rules form the foundation of their musical ability. They enable them to create harmony and melody. Once mastered, these rules become second nature, allowing the musician to improvise and innovate, and to express his or her unique artistic vision.

Similarly, the rules of Life serve as a foundation upon which we can build and create. When we embrace rules as tools rather than constraints, we unlock their potential to enhance our lives. Rules provide a framework within which we can explore, experiment and grow. They offer a sense of direction and purpose, guiding us toward our goals and aspirations. By understanding and mastering the rules, we gain the freedom to create better ones, to innovate and to transform our reality.

Understanding the rules of the Game is therefore the key to mastery. When we comprehend the principles and dynamics that govern our world, we are better equipped to navigate its challenges and seize its opportunities.

This understanding allows us to anticipate and adapt to change, to make informed decisions and to create strategies that align with our goals.

In appearance, rules and freedom may seem to be opposing forces. Rules provide structure and limitations, while freedom represents the ability to act without constraints. However, a deeper understanding reveals that these two concepts are interconnected and complementary.
What we call the "reconciliation of opposites".

Rules provide the foundation upon which freedom is built. They create a fairly stable and predictable environment that allows for exploration and innovation. Without rules, there would be chaos and uncertainty, making it difficult to achieve meaningful progress. Rules offer a sense of security and order, enabling us to focus our energy on creative pursuits.

Freedom, on the other hand, allows us to question and redefine the rules. It empowers us to challenge conventions and to envision new possibilities. Freedom fosters creativity and innovation, driving human progress and evolution. The interplay of rules and freedom creates a dynamic balance that fuels growth and transformation.

Here, there is no quick fix. Mastering the rules of the Game is a lifelong journey. It is a process of continuous learning, growth, and adaptation. Each stage of Life presents new challenges and opportunities, requiring us to refine our understanding and develop new skills.

This journey is not linear but cyclical. As we master one set of rules, we encounter new ones that challenge us to expand our knowledge and capabilities.

Each cycle of learning deepens our understanding and enhances our ability to create better rules. This iterative process is the essence of personal and collective evolution.

Along the way, we encounter mentors, peers and mentees that shape our journey. We learn from our successes and failures, from our joys and sorrows. Each experience contributes to our growth, enriching our understanding and empowering us to navigate the Game with greater insight.

Consider the field of science.

Scientists seek to understand the natural laws that govern the universe, from the motion of planets to the behavior of subatomic particles. Through observation, experimentation and analysis, they uncover the fundamental principles that shape our reality. This understanding not only advances human knowledge but also empowers us to harness these principles for practical applications, from technology and medicine to environmental conservation.

Think about it.

Every time an inventor comes up with a new invention, he has to challenge the established rules of the Game. He could never invent anything new if he stayed confined within the previous rules. What a successful inventor does is to use the old rules as a fondation to create new ones.

That is how our world is shaped.

All the time and everywhere.

Similarly, in our personal lives, understanding the rules of the Game enables us to make better choices.

As an example, when you understand the principles of nutrition and exercise, you can make decisions that promote your health, fitness and well-being.

When you understand the dynamics of relationships, you can cultivate meaningful connections and navigate conflicts with empathy and insight.

When you understand the principles of finance, you can manage your resources wisely and achieve financial stability.

It is the same in every area of Life.

If you don't understand something, you will never master it.

Eventually, the ultimate goal of mastering the rules of the Game is to create better ones. As you deepen your understanding and expand your skills, you gain the ability to innovate and transform your reality. You can challenge the status quo, question outdated assumptions and envision new possibilities. This creative power is the essence of human progress and evolution.

Creating better rules requires us to remain curious and open-minded, to seek new knowledge and perspectives.

It involves experimentation and risk-taking, the willingness to try new approaches and learn from failure. It demands resilience and perseverance, the capacity to overcome obstacles and setbacks.

Consider the pioneers and innovators who have reshaped our world throughout history. From the inventors of the wheel and the printing press, the light bulb and the plane, to the pioneers of the digital age and the internet, these individuals understood the existing rules and used that knowledge to create new ones. They saw beyond the limitations of their time, envisioning new possibilities and bringing them to life. Their contributions have transformed society, advancing human knowledge and improving our quality of life.

In our own lives, we can also harness this creative power to shape our destiny. By understanding the rules of the Game, we gain the confidence and competence to create new rules that align with our values and aspirations.

We can design our lives with intention and purpose, crafting a reality that reflects our true potential.

Therefore, education plays a crucial role in this process of mastering and creating rules. It is through education that we gain the knowledge and skills necessary to understand the world and navigate its complexities. Education equips us with the tools to think critically, to solve problems and to innovate.

However, true education extends beyond the confines of formal schooling. It is a lifelong journey of exploration and discovery. It involves not only constantly acquiring information but also developing wisdom and insight. It requires us to engage with the world with curiosity and openness, to learn from our experiences and from others.

The essential components of education are mentorship and guidance. By learning from those who have mastered the rules, we gain valuable insights and perspectives. Mentors offer guidance, support and encouragement, helping us to navigate our path and achieve our goals. They can also challenge us to think differently, to question our assumptions and to push beyond our limits.

In conclusion, learning the rules of the Grand Game will free you and empower you. And bring you to one of the most profound rewards : the joy of creation.

The ability to shape your reality, to bring your visions to life, is a deeply fulfilling and empowering experience. It is through creation that you express your unique gifts and contributions, leaving a lasting impact on the world.

However, creation is not limited to grand achievements or monumental projects.

It is found in the everyday acts of innovation and transformation. It is in the way we solve problems, the way we nurture relationships, the way we grow wiser.

The way we pursue our passions.

RULE 5

*"The only part of the Game you can truly control
is your MIND."*

Life is 1 % what happens to you and 99 % how you react to it. Take a minute to reflect upon it.

As you journey through this Game, you will encounter countless situations that elude your grasp and circumstances beyond your control.
It is evident that while you might influence your surroundings to a degree, true mastery lies not in controlling the external world but in governing your internal realm.
Your MIND.

This realization, profound in its simplicity, holds the key to navigating the vicissitudes of Life with peace and balance.
In other words, your MIND is your greatest asset in the Grand Game of Life. It is the control center for your thoughts, emotions, and actions, in that order.
Therefore, by mastering your MINDset, you will gain control over your responses to external events and challenges. You won't be able to control them, but it won't matter because you will control how you react to them, which is the essential part.
How to get there can be sum up in one single sentence.
From the beginning of time, it seems that the most fundamental message that all wise men and women, and all great teachers from various spiritual traditions and religions, has been, put in its most simple way :

"You become what you think about."

As infants, thrust into a world of unpredictability, we rely entirely on those around us to meet our needs. As we grow, we gradually acquire skills and knowledge, gaining a semblance of control over our environment. We learn to walk, speak, read, and write, mastering the basics of existence. Yet, as we mature, we come to understand that the scope of our control is limited.

Consider the natural world—weather patterns, the passage of time, the behavior of all beings. These elements, fundamental to our experience, lie beyond our influence. We can prepare for a storm, but we cannot prevent it. We can nurture relationships, but we cannot dictate someone else's feelings or actions. This understanding often arrives with a sense of discomfort, for we often crave certainty and stability in an ever changing world.

The notion of control is, in many ways, an illusion. We build routines, set goals and create structures in an attempt to impose order upon chaos. Yet, Life has a way of reminding us of its inherent unpredictability.

This dance with uncertainty is not a sign of failure but a testament to the dynamic nature of existence.

Amidst this unpredictability however, lies one domain where we hold true power: our MIND. The MIND, with its boundless capacity for thought, emotion and perception, is the seat of our experience. It is through the MIND that we interpret and respond to the world around us. While we may not control the events that befall us, we can choose how we react to them.

This choice is both a privilege and a responsibility.

Our reactions shape our reality, influencing our emotions, actions, and ultimately, our destiny. The MIND is a powerful tool, capable of transforming challenges into opportunities, pain into growth and fear into courage. By mastering our

MIND, we gain the ability to navigate Life's uncertainties with resilience and wisdom.

Perception is the lens through which we view the world.
It is shaped by our attitude, beliefs and experiences.
Two individuals can encounter the same event and perceive it in entirely different ways. This difference in perception underscores the power of the MIND in shaping our reality.

Consider a dramatic event. An accident.
To some people, it might become the event that plunge them in depression and despair, breaking their spirits. To others, it may represent an opportunity for change and growth, bringing them a new purpose. The external event remains the same, but the internal response varies, highlighting the subjective nature of experience, as well as the true absolute power that lies in each and every one of us.

This power of perception extends to all aspects of Life.
Challenges and setbacks, while often perceived as negative, can be reframed as opportunities for growth and learning. Successes and achievements, rather than being taken for granted, can be viewed with gratitude and humility.
By consciously shaping our perceptions, we cultivate a mindset that is resilient, optimistic and empowered.

Again, mindfulness, the practice of bringing your awareness to the present moment, without judgment or distraction, will be a powerful tool for mastering your MIND, enabling you to observe your thoughts and emotions with clarity and detachment. Through mindfulness, we develop the ability to respond to Life with intention rather than react impulsively. It involves paying attention to our inner experience—our thoughts, feelings and bodily sensations. By cultivating this awareness, we gain insight into the patterns and habits that shape our reactions. We learn to recognize the triggers that evoke stress, anger or fear, and to respond with calmness and confidence.

Take the example of anger.

When we are mindful, we can observe the sensation of anger arising within us—the increased heart rate, the tension in our muscles, the racing thoughts. Rather than being swept away by this emotion, we can take a step back, breathe deeply and choose a measured response. This practice of mindfulness transforms our relationship with our emotions, empowering us to act with wisdom and compassion.

The choice is ours.

Life presents us with a myriad of experiences, both pleasant and challenging. It is our choice to embrace all aspects of our journey, recognizing that each moment, whether joyful or painful, is a part of the larger tapestry of existence. By accepting what we cannot change, we free ourselves from the burden of resistance and open ourselves to growth and transformation. Our attitude—the way we approach and interpret Life's events—plays a determining role in shaping our experience. A positive attitude fosters resilience, creativity and well-being, while a negative attitude can lead to frustration, stagnation and despair. By making the conscious choice of always having a positive attitude, no matter the circumstances, we enhance our ability to navigate Life's challenges with effectiveness and appreciation.

A positive attitude is not about denying reality or ignoring difficulties though. It is about approaching Life with a sense of possibility and hope, recognizing that we have the power to shape our responses and create positive outcomes. No matter what. It involves focusing on solutions rather than problems, on opportunities rather than obstacles. Even in the most dire circumstances, individuals have the power to choose their attitude. This choice is the essence of human freedom. By finding meaning in your suffering, you will transform your experience.

The simple act of waking up each morning and expressing gratitude for the gift of a new day, will set a positive tone for the day ahead. By appreciating the beauty of nature, the kindness of others, and the opportunities before us, we enhance our sense of well-being and resilience.

You might start wondering :
"Does it also apply to the most important thing in Life?
Does it apply to happiness?
It seems like we can't control it.
It just comes and goes like the weather."
The truth is, happiness is a choice.
You can only be happy, or successful, or rich, if you chose so.
Therefore, make a choice and commit to it.

You will become what you think about.

Where to start?
The answer is : imagination and visualization.

They are the most powerful tools of the MIND for shaping your reality. They involve creating a mental image of your desired outcome and focusing your energy and intention on bringing it to life.

By using your imagination and practicing visualization, you enhance your ability to manifest your goals and dreams.

Visualization involves using your imagination to create a vivid and detailed picture of your desired outcome. It is a practice of aligning your thoughts, emotions and actions with your vision. By focusing on this positive image, you attract the resources and opportunities needed to bring it to fruition.

This is a wild Game we play, and you will not always be master of your circumstances. However, by learning to control your MIND, you will maintain inner peace and clarity regardless of external events.

Master your thoughts, and you will master your emotions.
Master your emotions, and you will master your actions.
Therefore, however tough and unpredictable, Life will always be 1 % what happens to you, and 99 % what you make of it.

By mastering your MIND, you will master your Life.

Once again, you are what you think about.
So what do you think about? Deep, deep down.
Consciously or unconsciously, how do you think of yourself?
Do you see yourself as sad? Broken? Depressed?
Alcoholic or heavy smoker?
Overweight and lacking energy?
Angry or jealous? Poor and greedy?

Or do you see yourself as beautiful, fit, joyful, humble, rich or generous? Happy, healthy, wealthy?

Today, I want you to reinvent yourself and to imagine the best possible version of yourself. Think about the best possible version of you. Then, describe that person in a few words.

And finally, remember these words and focus on them.
Everyday. Every hour. Every minute if you can.

No matter what happens, no matter the circumstances, keep focusing on these few words. The best version of yourself.

And your life will be transformed.

RULE 6

*"Within the Game,
your potential is always infinite."*

Sooner or later, limiting thoughts will appear :
"All this is great but... it is not for me.
I wish I could but I can't.
I can't because there is this or that in my life that prevents me
from achieving what I dream to be.
It prevents me from being the person I want to be.
Because of this or that, I feel limited."
You might be missing an arm, or the use of your legs.
You might be blind.
You might be dyslexic.
You might be depressed or penniless.
Nevertheless, your potential is still endless.

Each of us has limitations, may they be physical, mental or spiritual. But the Grand Game of Life is so diverse and rich, and involves so many layers, so many possible actions, reactions, consequences and outcomes, that no matter your situation and how limited it might seem, possibilities are always infinite.

In the grand theater of Life, each of us plays a unique role, navigating through a world that is vast, complex and endlessly rich. Regardless of our circumstances, the possibilities available to us are boundless.

The essence of our journey lies in understanding that within the Game, our potential is always infinite. This realization, profound and liberating, invites us to explore the depths of our being and the limitless opportunities that Life presents.

Our potential is never confined by our current circumstances or limitations. It is a dynamic force that evolves and expands as we grow and learn. Each experience, whether positive or negative, contributes to our development, shaping us into more capable and resilient beings.

By embracing this potential, we open ourselves to a world of endless possibilities.

From the dawn of human existence, our species has demonstrated an extraordinary capacity for adaptation, growth, innovation, and transformation. Our journey from primitive beings to the architects of advanced civilizations is a testament to the boundless potential of the human spirit.

This potential is not limited to a selected few; it resides within each of us, waiting to be discovered and actualized.

The natural world, with its awe-inspiring beauty and complexity, is a testament to the infinite possibilities that surround us. From the vastness of the oceans to the intricacies of a single leaf, from the bottom of the sea to the top of the highest mountains, nature reveals the boundless creativity of Life. By observing and learning from nature, we gain insights into our own potential and the limitless opportunities available to us.

Consider the evolution of human progress: the creation of written language, the construction of temples, the rise of mighty empires, the circumnavigation of the Earth, the exploration of space. Each of these milestones was achieved by individuals who dared to imagine the impossible and to push the boundaries of what was known. These visionaries were not inherently different from us; they simply tapped into the infinite potential that lies within all of us.

Life offers an abundance of opportunities for exploration and growth. The world is rich with diverse cultures, landscapes, and experiences. Each thread represents a unique possibility, a new path to be explored. This diversity is a source of countless avenues for personal and collective development.

Human culture, with its myriad expressions of art, science, and philosophy, further illustrates the infinite potential within the Game of Life. Each culture offers a unique perspective, a different way of understanding and interacting with the world. By learning about other cultures, we expand our horizons and enrich our own experience, tapping into the collective wisdom of humanity.

Remember the story of individuals who have overcome great adversity to achieve remarkable success. These individuals did not allow their circumstances to define them; instead, they used their inner strength to pursue their dreams. Their stories remind us that our potential is not limited by our circumstances, but by our willingness to persevere and to believe in ourselves.

Which path will YOU explore amongst these endless possibilities? Which one will be yours?

Your imagination is the gateway to your infinite potential.

It is through imagination that we envision new possibilities and create new realities. Our ability to imagine allows us to transcend our current circumstances and to explore the vast landscape of potential that lies beyond the horizon.

The role of imagination in the creative process that artists, writers and musicians go through. They draw upon their imagination to create works that inspire and transform. Scientists and inventors use their imagination to envision new solutions and innovations. In every field of human endeavor, imagination is the spark that ignites the flame of potential.

Look everywhere around you.
Everything you see, the roads, the buildings and the parcs, the furniture, the paintings and the books, the glass you hold in your hand, the chair you sit on, all of this was, at some point, nothing but an idea in someone's MIND.

That is the power of an idea.
The power of a seed.
It starts in your MIND, then appears on the paper.
And eventually becomes a reality.

Finally, imagination is not limited to the realm of creativity; it is a fundamental aspect of human experience. It allows us to dream, to aspire and to envision a better future. By cultivating our imagination, we unlock the power to shape our destiny.

The journey of self-discovery is a path to realizing our infinite potential. It involves exploring the depths of our being, uncovering our strengths and weaknesses, and embracing our true selves.

This journey is not an easy one, but it is essential for unlocking the boundless possibilities within us.

Self-discovery requires us to look within, to reflect on our experiences, and to seek understanding and growth. It involves questioning our beliefs, challenging our assumptions, as well as confronting our fears. By embarking on this journey, we gain insight into our true nature and the ever flowing source of potential that resides within us.

When we embrace our true selves, we gain the confidence and clarity to pursue our passions and aspirations.

It is a journey of empowerment.
A path to realizing our infinite potential.

So, what is stopping you?
In the majority of cases, our perceived identity feels limited because we keep focusing on a dark past. We still allow our past, this illusion of the MIND, to entrap us and define who we are or can be. As long as you won't free yourself from that illusion, it will limit your potential, building a version of yourself you are not sure you still want to be.

Remember : "You are what you think about."
Do you feel that your past is still dictating who you are?
Then take back control.

Start by being in the HERE and NOW.
The first thing you will feel is probably gratitude.
Gratitude for everything you have and everything you are.

In the present, you are perfect.

From that place of peace, let your imagination make you envision new horizons. Feel your infinite potential.
Discover a new identity. A new YOU.

And this new YOU is sitting in a positive future, waiting for you to join. Anytime. It is just a short step.

The two of you were always meant to meet.

Eventually, a shift will happen.
A shift of identity from the dark past to the positive future.
A future of joy and laughter, of beauty and harmony.
A Life of love and abundance.

One last time, remember : "You are what you think about."

If all you think of is the best version of yourself and a positive vision of the future, that is what you will become.

That is who you will be.

RULE 7

*"You can achieve
absolutely everything you want."*

Everything you want.
Everything you can dream of.
Everything.

Since you shifted your MINDset from :
"Why I can't get this" to "How I can get it."
You are now ready to explore the "how" part.
It is maybe the most exciting part.
So how?

There is a formula.
In the Grand Game of Life, this formula will allow you to acquire anything you want and desire, without being selfish and without violating the rights of others.

The formula follows these 3 simple steps.
The difficulty lies in their execution.

I.   Know exactly what you want.
II. Put all your ressources in achieving your goals.
III. Never give up.

The notion that we can achieve absolutely everything we want is not merely a motivational aphorism; it is a profound truth woven in the very fabric of our being. The universe, vast and abundant, offers endless possibilities to those who dare to dream and act with unwavering determination. To harness this potential, one must adhere to three fundamental steps. They are very simple to understand but very hard to execute.

That is because these steps, though simple in concept, require a depth of commitment and resilience that transforms the aspirant into the master of his fate. Let's go through them.

I. Know EXACTLY what you want.

The first step towards achieving anything you desire is to possess a clear and unwavering vision of your goal. This clarity acts as a beacon, a compass, guiding your actions and decisions with precision and purpose. Without a clear destination, the journey is aimless, and the energy dissipates into the void of indecision.

Most people don't know what they truly want.
They "kind of" want something.
But they don't know EXACTLY what they want.

If it is money you want, how much?
Take a piece of paper and write it down.

Even better, take the time of imagining the lifestyle you want, then calculate how much that would cost you every year.
Be large in your estimation, then write that number down.

If it is a car, which one?
Which model? Which year? Which features?

If it is a house, draw it on the paper.
Search for what you dream of online and take screenshots.
Where would it be on the map? Which country? Which city?
Which exact location on the coast or in the mountains?

If it is a relationship that you want, how would that look like and how would that feel?
How about safe, trustful and caring?
Or spicy, passionate and a bit crazy?

What would that partner be like? The ideal partner?
Write it down. How about children? How would they be?
Write it down.

If it is a new identity you want for yourself, how would you reinvent yourself? In details.
Maybe "always calm and caring, selfless and generous, funny and beautiful, rich and in good shape?"
Why not?

Remember, your potential is infinite.
Here, you are only limited by your own imagination
and self-imposed limits.
In other words, there are no limits.

When you know exactly what you want, you align your thoughts, emotions and actions towards that singular objective. This alignment creates a harmonious resonance between your inner world and the external universe, drawing opportunities and resources towards you as if by magnetic force. Knowing exactly what you want requires deep introspection and honesty.

It is not enough to pursue goals imposed by societal expectations or superficial desires. True clarity comes from within, from a place of authenticity and self-awareness. Take time to explore your passions, your values, and your dreams.

What ignites your spirit?
What brings you a deep sense of fulfillment and joy?
These are the questions that will lead you to your true desires.

II. Put ALL your resources into achieving your goals.

Once you have a clear vision of your goal, the next step is to commit fully to its realization. This commitment involves dedicating all your resources—time, energy, skills, and even your very being—towards achieving your objective.
It is a total immersion in the pursuit of your dream, a wholehearted embrace of the journey.

The notion of putting all your resources into achieving your goals is not merely about working harder; it is about working smarter, with focus and intentionality. It is about aligning every aspect of your life with your goal, creating a synergy that propels you forward with unstoppable momentum.

This step requires discipline and perseverance. It involves making sacrifices and prioritizing your goals above immediate gratification.

It means waking up each day with a sense of purpose and dedication, taking consistent action towards your dream, no matter how small the steps may seem. Each action, no matter how trivial, accumulates over time and advances you towards the realization of your vision.

Consider the example of great artists, scientists and entrepreneurs. Their achievements were not the result of sporadic efforts, but of sustained and focused dedication. They immersed themselves in their craft, sharpening their skills, and continually pushing the boundaries of what was possible. Their success was a testament to the power of commitment and the relentless pursuit of their goals.

III. NEVER give up.

Persistence is the cornerstone of success.

The final step in achieving anything you desire is perhaps the most challenging, the quality that separates those who achieve their dreams from those who fall short.
It is the unwavering determination to keep moving forward, even in the face of obstacles, setbacks and failures, because the journey towards your goal will inevitably be fraught with challenges. There will be moments of doubt and frustration.
There will be times when the path seems insurmountable and the dream distant. In these moments, the strength of your commitment and the depth of your resilience will be tested.

To never give up is to embrace the journey in its entirety, to recognize that setbacks and failures are not the end, but merely part of the process. Each obstacle is an opportunity for growth, each failure a lesson in disguise.
By viewing challenges through this lens, you transform adversity into a catalyst for progress.

Resilience is the key to never giving up.

It is the ability to bounce back from setbacks, to maintain your focus and determination in the face of adversity.

Think of individuals who achieved great success despite overwhelming odds. Their journeys were marked by persistence and resilience. They faced numerous failures and rejections, yet they never gave up. Their extraordinary determination eventually led to breakthroughs and triumphs that seemed impossible at the outset. Their stories serve as a reminder that the power to achieve anything lies within each of us, if we are willing to persevere and never give up.

Sadly, that is not what most people do.
First, the vast majority of the population actually don't know what they really want.
Sometimes they think they do, but their goals are vague and there is nothing precise or detailed about them.

Ask yourself :
How would you ever get what you want, if you don't know exactly what it is? What would be the odds of you arriving at destination, a precise location on the globe, if you didn't even know where you wanted to go?

Secondly, some people put immense ressources into achieving something, into a relationship, into their job or their house.
But they are not even sure that is EXACTLY what they want.
Maybe it is the wrong goal? The wrong person, job or house?

Next, you will notice that most people around you only "kind of" know what they want, but on top of that, they put very little ressources into it.

"I want to write a book" they say.
But they don't put any real time and effort into it.

An entire year later, only a few draft pages are written.

"I want to learn a new language" they say.
But they never fully immerse themselves into that language and into the learning process. Years later, that goal ends up on a large pile of unachieved dreams.

Finally, it is common to see people somehow knowing what they want, putting important ressources into reaching their goals but at the first obstacle, they give up.
At the first setback or the first difficulty, they get discouraged and fall back on that belief that "If it doesn't go perfectly, then it is not meant to be. It is too difficult. It is impossible."

Consider someone that would dream of sailing across the ocean from northern latitudes to a tropical island that lies on the Equator. What an amazing adventure that would be!

What if they actually didn't know exactly which harbour they should head to? Which coordinates to enter on the GPS?
What if they didn't invest in a solid, well-equipped boat?
What if they didn't learn how to sail the high seas? What if they didn't train to know how to react in emergencies?
Finally, what if they were turning back at the first storm?
At the first broken sail? At the first sleepless night?
What would be their chances to actually get to that dream island they thought of?

None. Zero.
They would never get there alive.

That is why the 3 steps of the formula work together.

They are interconnected and mutually reinforcing each other.
Each step builds upon the other, creating a powerful framework for achieving your dreams. They are not easy to stick to. But if you respect them, you will be unstoppable and sooner or later, you will reach your destination.
By embracing these steps, you align your thoughts, emotions, and actions with your true desires. This alignment creates a powerful synergy that propels you forward. It transforms the pursuit of your dreams from a daunting challenge into a joyful journey of self-discovery and growth.

Underlying these steps is the power of belief.
Belief in yourself, in your dreams, and in the infinite possibilities of the universe. Belief is not a passive state; it is an active force that shapes your reality.
When you believe in your ability to achieve your dreams, you create a self-fulfilling prophecy.

Your thoughts, emotions and actions align with this belief, creating a positive feedback loop that sets you up for success.

It is like the placebo effect in medicine.
When patients believe in the efficacy of a treatment, they often experience real improvements in their health, even if the treatment itself is inert.
This phenomenon illustrates the profound impact of belief on our physical and psychological well-being.

Similarly, when you believe in your potential to achieve your dreams, you activate a powerful force that enhances your capabilities and drives you towards your objectives.

You now have at our disposal some of the most powerful tools the human mind possesses. You are now aware of how to unleash you infinite potential and how to become the engineer of your life.

This comes with a warning.

With increased knowledge comes increased power.
With increased power comes increased responsibility.

Your MIND is a double-edged sword.
It never stops working and can be used 2 ways.

It can work to your benefit or to your detriment.
You can use that power to design, create and enjoy the life you've always dreamed of. Your best possible life.

But the reverse is also true.

If you can't control your MIND and misuse it, you could create, or keep creating, design and then hate, your worst possible life.

The choice is in your hands.
Or, more accurately, the choice is in your MIND.

Ultimately, be aware that the pursuit of your dreams is not just about achieving the end result, but about embracing the journey itself. It is about finding joy and fulfillment in the process of growth, learning and self-discovery.
The journey is where true transformation occurs, where you become the person capable of achieving your dreams.
If you focus on experiencing the joy of the journey, you shift your perspective from a destination-oriented mindset to a process-oriented one. This shift will transform the pursuit of your goals from a source of stress and pressure into a source of inspiration, joy, fulfillment and grace.

The journey is the reward.
Not the destination.

RULE 8

*"Always be grateful for what you receive,
and generous in what you give."*

You can get it all.
You will get it all.
Health, money, fame, power, love, happiness.
All the greatest things Life has to offer.
But if you don't appreciate them and if you don't share them,
they will simply be worthless.

This is the last rule, not the least.
Without it, the other 7 rules would be incomplete.

The more you receive, the more you should give.
The more you give, the more you should receive.

In the vast symphony of existence lies a profound truth which resonates with the harmony of the cosmos: the principle of Gratitude and Generosity. The 2 G's.

"Always be grateful for what you receive, and generous in what you give" is not merely a moral directive, but a path to living in tune with the universal rhythm.

Gratitude is the recognition of the abundance in our lives.

It is the conscious appreciation of the gifts, both big and small, that we receive each day. In a world often focused on lack and scarcity, gratitude shifts our perspective to one of abundance and fulfillment. It allows us to see the beauty and wonder in the ordinary, transforming the mundane into the miraculous.

When we express gratitude, we acknowledge the interdependence of all things. We recognize that we are not isolated beings, but part of a larger web of relationships and interactions. Everything we receive is a result of this interconnectedness, a gift from the universe that supports and sustains us. By being grateful, we honor this interconnectedness and align ourselves with the flow of Life.

Let's set this straight.
Gratitude is not about complacency or passivity.

It does not mean that we should accept everything that comes our way without striving for more. Rather, it is about recognizing and appreciating what we have, while also aspiring to grow, thrive and evolve. Gratitude grounds us in the present moment, providing a foundation of contentment from which we can pursue our dreams and aspirations.

Gratitude is a natural extension of mindfulness, as it involves being fully present to the gifts and blessings in our lives.
By cultivating gratitude, we enhance our mindfulness and deepen our connection to the present moment.

Generosity is the act of giving freely and selflessly.
It is an expression of love, compassion and empathy towards others. When we are generous, we share our resources—time, energy, knowledge and material wealth—with those around us. Generosity is a manifestation of our interconnectedness, a way of contributing to the well-being of others and enriching the collective experience of Life.

Generosity is not about the quantity of what we give, but the quality of our intention. It is not measured by the size of our contributions, but by the spirit in which we offer them.

True generosity comes from a place of abundance, a recognition that by giving, we are not losing something, but participating in the flow of Life.
The truth is, when we give generously, we open ourselves to receive even more, as the act of giving creates a positive feedback loop of abundance and gratitude.

You should be like a flowing river.
A river does not hoard its water; it comes and flows freely, nourishing the land and the life forms it encounters. In return, it is replenished by the rains and the melting snows.
Similarly, when we give generously, we keep the flow of Life moving, creating a cycle of giving and receiving that sustains and enriches all involved.

Gratitude and Generosity are two sides of the same coin.
They are complementary forces that enhance and reinforce each other. When we are grateful for what we receive, we naturally feel a desire to give back, to share our blessings with others. Conversely, when we are generous in what we give, we cultivate a deeper sense of gratitude, as we recognize the abundance in our lives and the joy of contributing to the well-being of others.

This interplay creates a virtuous cycle of abundance and satisfaction. If you express gratitude, you will attract more blessings into your life.
If you give generously, you will create a flow of positive energy that enriches both yourself and those around us.
This cycle is a reflection of the universal Law of Reciprocity, the principle that what you put out into the world returns to you in kind.

Take the example of the farmer who plants seeds in the ground. He does not lock the seeds in a safe, but brings them out to the open field and plants them with care and intention in order to create abundance.

By doing this, he actually takes a risk.

But the reward is worth the risk. As he tends to the growing plants, he expresses gratitude for the fertile soil, the sun and the rain. In time, the seeds grow into a bountiful harvest, providing nourishment for the farmer and his community, as well as new seeds for the years to come. The act of planting the seeds is an act of generosity, and the resulting harvest is a source of gratitude. This cycle of giving and receiving sustains forever the farmer and the land, creating a harmonious balance of abundance.

There are a few very simple ways to start integrating these principles into your daily life.

Start a gratitude journal.

Each day, take a few moments to write down 3 things you are grateful for. These can be simple things, such as a warm cup of coffee in the morning sun, a kind word from a friend, the joy that your spouse and children bring into your life, or the beauty of a sunset. By consistently acknowledging the good around you, you cultivate a habit of gratitude that enhances your overall well-being and outlook on life.

Practice acts of generosity, both big and small.

Offer a smile to a stranger.

Lend a helping hand to a neighbor.

Give your spare change to the homeless in the street.

Volunteer your time to a cause you care about.

When you give, do so with an open heart and a sense of joy, without expecting anything in return, since true generosity is not about the size of the gift, but the intention behind it.

Embrace the idea of "paying it forward."
When you receive a kindness or a blessing, find a way to pass it on to someone else. This creates a ripple effect of positive energy that extends beyond your immediate circle, contributing to the well-being of the larger community.
By paying it forward, you honor the interconnectedness of all things and participate in the flow of Life.

Gratitude and generosity are not merely ethical practices; they are also spiritual principles that connect us to the divine.

In many spiritual traditions, gratitude is seen as a form of prayer, a way of acknowledging the presence and blessings of the divine in our lives. Generosity, likewise, is viewed as a sacred act, a way of expressing love and compassion towards others. By cultivating gratitude and generosity, we align ourselves with the higher vibrations of love and compassion. These practices elevate our consciousness and deepen our connection to the divine. They remind us that we are not separate beings, but part of a larger, interconnected whole. In this way, gratitude and generosity become pathways to spiritual growth and enlightenment.

You will find this principle in the teachings of various spiritual traditions. In Buddhism, the practice of generosity is one of the foundational principles of the path to Enlightenment. By giving freely and selflessly, practitioners cultivate a sense of detachment from material possessions and develop qualities of compassion and loving kindness.

Similarly, in Christianity, gratitude is emphasized as a way of recognizing and honoring God's blessings.

These spiritual teachings remind us that gratitude and generosity are not just moral obligations, but profound practices that transform our lives and elevate our consciousness. By embracing these principles, we align ourselves with the divine flow of love and abundance, creating a life of deeper meaning and ultimate fulfillment.

Start to express gratitude regularly to your spouse or partner and you will see how gratitude and generosity have a profound impact on your relationships.
Observe how he or she will transform just by receiving your appreciation, your "I noticed you did this for me and I really appreciate it. Thank you. I'm so happy to have you in my life."
It will strengthen your bond and create a positive atmosphere of appreciation and respect because gratitude fosters a sense of connection and belonging, enhancing the quality of our interactions and deepening our relationships.

Generosity, likewise, enriches our relationships by fostering a spirit of cooperation and mutual support.
Notice the impact of gratitude and generosity in a family setting, if you start rendering acts of service on a regular basis.

Try with very simple things, with your kids for example.
"Today, I made your favourite cake." or "I saw your bike was broken so I took care of it."

The impact of gratitude and generosity extends beyond our immediate relationships and communities. These practices create a ripple effect that touches the lives of many.

We all know the story of a single act of kindness that sparks a chain reaction of generosity. A person buys a cup of coffee for a stranger, who is so touched by the gesture that they decide to pay it forward by helping someone else. This act of kindness spreads, creating a wave of positive energy that impacts countless people. This ripple effect demonstrates the power of gratitude and generosity to create a more compassionate and connected world.

By embracing gratitude and generosity, we contribute to the collective well-being of humanity. We create a culture of appreciation and giving, where individuals are inspired to support and uplift each other. This culture of gratitude and generosity fosters a sense of global unity and brotherhood, promoting peace and harmony in the world.

In the Game of Life, we are both givers and receivers, constantly exchanging energy, time, love and resources. This dance is a reflection of the cosmic order, where everything is interconnected and in constant motion. By embracing this dance, we find our place in the grand tapestry of existence, contributing to the harmony and beauty of the whole.

In this exchange lies the true essence of success.
Gratitude transforms even the smallest blessings into moments of joy, while generosity enriches both the receiver and the giver. When you give of your wealth, of your time, of your happiness, they multiply, creating a ripple effect that touches countless lives.

Remember, success is not a solitary pursuit.
Its truest form is found in the connections we forge and the kindness we extend.

As we journey through Life, let us appreciate the gifts and blessings we receive and share them freely with others.

Let us tap into the infinite potential of the universe and create a thriving life.

It doesn't matter how much is given to you if you don't appreciate it, and whatever you receive is meant to be shared. There is no happiness, and no succes, but shared.

By being grateful for what you receive and generous in what you give, you align yourself with the universal rhythm and create a life of joy and abundance.

So embrace this final rule, and let the Grand Game of Life unfold in all its beauty and splendor.

CONCLUSION

The journey of understanding yourself and the world around you is a wonderful adventure, and an intricate game.
This Grand Game of Life is guided by principles that, when followed, illuminate the path to a Life of meaning, happiness and success. And keep in mind that success is not measured by material wealth or social status.
But by the fulfillment and the joy you experience.

These 8 rules offer a collective framework for understanding the Game of Life and your role within it.

They are not just abstract concepts.
They are practical tools and guidelines that, when internalized and practiced, offer profound insights into the human experience and lead you to freedom.
These 8 rules serve as the keys which will empower you to navigate the complexities of the world with grace and wisdom, and, revealing the interconnectedness of all things, will unlock the mysteries of a Life of Abundance.

They are new ideas now implanted in your MIND.

The seeds have been sown.
If your nurture them, they will grow into wonderful plants of which you will one day reap the fruits.